JESUS CHRIST SUPERSTAR

LYRICS by TIM RICE
MUSIC by ANDREW LLOYD WEBBER

CONTENTS

ISBN 0-88188-541-X

HAL•LEONARD®
CORPORATION

7777 W. BLUEMOUND RD. P.O. BOX 13819 MILWAUKEE, WI 53213

Visit Hal Leonard Online at
www.halleonard.com

CAST

THE SINGERS, IN THE ORDER OF
THEIR APPEARANCE:

JUDAS ISCARIOT
JESUS CHRIST
MARY MAGDALENE
PRIEST
CAIAPHAS, HIGH PRIEST
ANNAS
SIMON ZEALOTES
PONTIUS PILATE
MAID BY THE FIRE
PETER
KING HEROD

OTHER SINGERS (APOSTLES, PRIESTS,
ROMAN SOLDIERS,
MERCHANTS, CROWDS, ETC.)

HEAVEN ON THEIR MINDS

Words by TIM RICE
Music by ANDREW LLOYD WEBBER

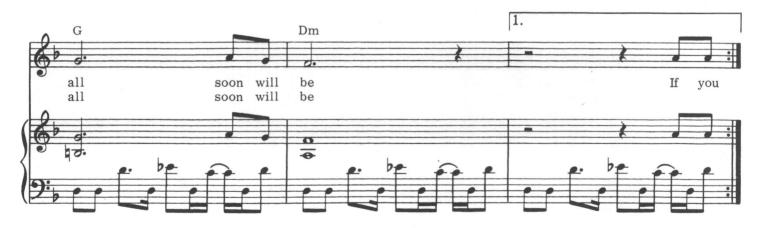

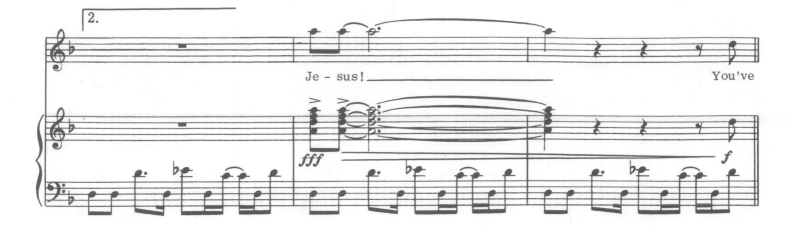

Je - sus! _____ You've

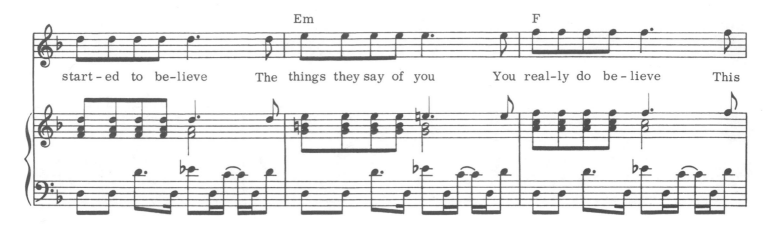

start - ed to be-lieve The things they say of you You real-ly do be-lieve This

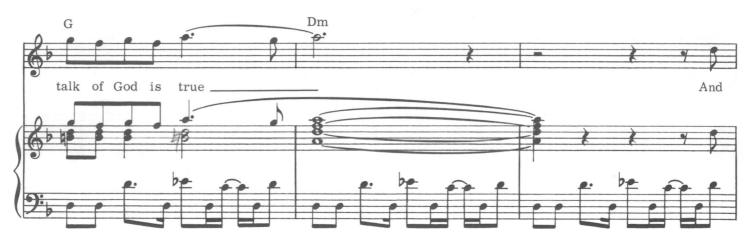

talk of God is true _____ And

all the good you've done will soon get swept a - way

You've be-gun to mat-ter more_ than_ the things you say _____

Lis-ten Je - sus I don't like what I see _____ All I ask is that you
I re-mem-ber when this whole thing be-gan _____ No talk of God then we

lis - ten to me And re - mem-ber — I've been your right hand man_
called you a man And be - lieve me — my ad - mi - ra - tion for you

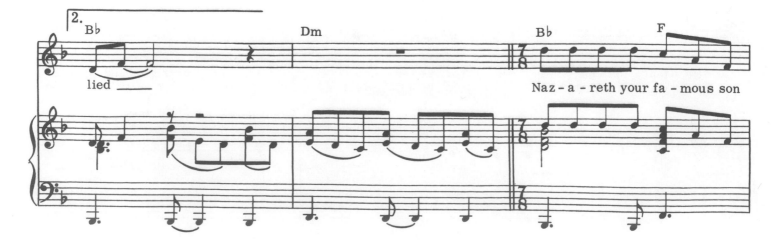

should have stayed a great un-known Like his fa-ther carv-ing wood—

he'd have made good   Ta-bles, chairs and oak-en chests would have suit-ed Je-sus best

He'd have caused no-bod-y harm— no-one a-larm

Lis-ten Je-sus do you care for your race?__   Don't you see we must
Lis-ten Je-sus to the warn-ing I give __   Please re-mem-ber that I

WHAT'S THE BUZZ

Bethany, Friday night

APOSTLES

What's the buzz? Tell me what's happening

JESUS

Why should you want to know?
Don't you mind about the future, don't you try
   to think ahead
Save tomorrow for tomorrow, think about today instead

APOSTLES

What's the buzz? Tell me what's happening

JESUS

I could give you facts and figures—I could give you plans
   and forecasts
Even tell you where I'm going—

APOSTLES

When do we ride into Jerusalem?

JESUS

Why should you want to know?
Why are you obsessed with fighting times and fates
   you can't defy?
If you knew the path we're riding you'd understand it
   less than I

APOSTLES

What's the buzz? Tell me what's happening

MARY MAGDALENE

Let me try to cool down your face a bit

JESUS

That feels nice, so nice...
Mary that is good—
While you prattle through your supper—where and when
   and who and how
She alone has tried to give me what I need
   right here and now

APOSTLES

What's the buzz? Tell me what's happening?

STRANGE THING MYSTIFYING

JUDAS

It seems to me a strange thing, mystifying
That a man like you can waste his time
 on women of her kind
Yes I can understand that she amuses
But to let her stroke you, kiss your hair, is hardly in your line

It's not that I object to her profession
But she doesn't fit in well with what you teach and say
It doesn't help us if you're inconsistent
They only need a small excuse to put us all away

JESUS

Who are you to criticise her? Who are you to despise her?
Leave her, leave her, let her be now
Leave her, leave her, she's with me now
If your slate is clean—then you can throw stones
If your slate is not then leave her alone
I'm amazed that men like you can be
 so shallow thick and slow
There is not a man among you who knows
 or cares if I come or go

ALL (SAVE JUDAS)

No you're wrong! You're very wrong!
 How can you say that?

JESUS

Not one—not one of you!

EVERYTHING'S ALRIGHT

Words by TIM RICE
Music by ANDREW LLOYD WEBBER

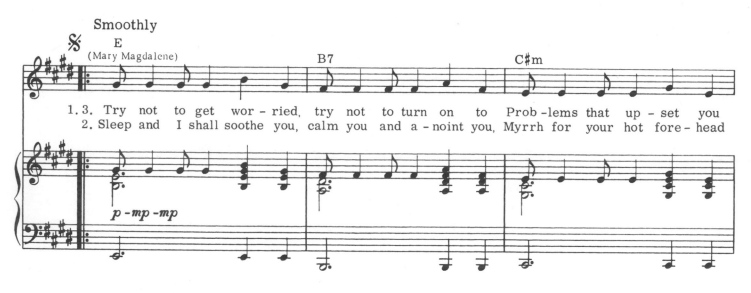

1.3. Try not to get wor-ried, try not to turn on to Prob-lems that up-set you
2. Sleep and I shall soothe you, calm you and a-noint you, Myrrh for your hot fore-head

oh   don't you know Ev-'ry-thing's al-right yes ev-'ry-thing's fine   And we
oh   then you'll feel Ev-'ry-thing's al-right yes ev-'ry-thing's fine   And it's

want you to sleep well to - night _____ Let the world_ turn with-out you to -
cool_ and the oint-ment's sweet _____ For the fire_ in your head and

night _____ If we try we'll get by so for - get all a - bout us to -
feet _____ Close your eyes close your eyes And re - lax think of noth - ing to -

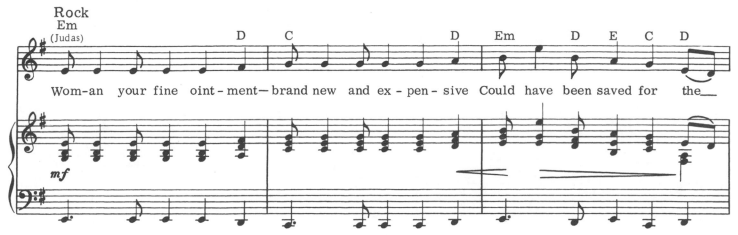

(Apostles' Women)

night _____
night _____
Ev - 'ry - thing's al - right yes ev - 'ry - thing's al - right yes

Rock

(Judas)

Wom-an your fine oint-ment—brand new and ex - pen - sive Could have been saved for the_

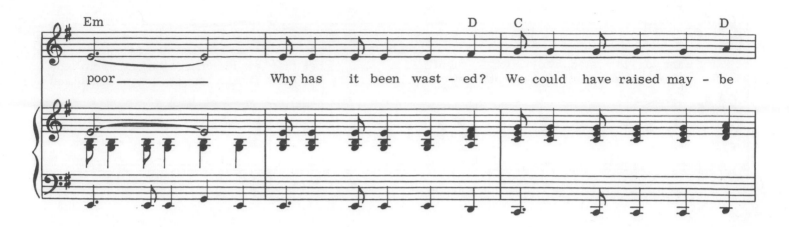

poor _____ Why has it been wast-ed? We could have raised may-be

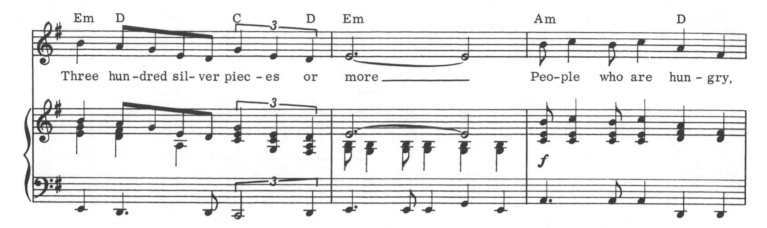

Three hun-dred sil-ver piec-es or more _____ Peo-ple who are hun-gry,

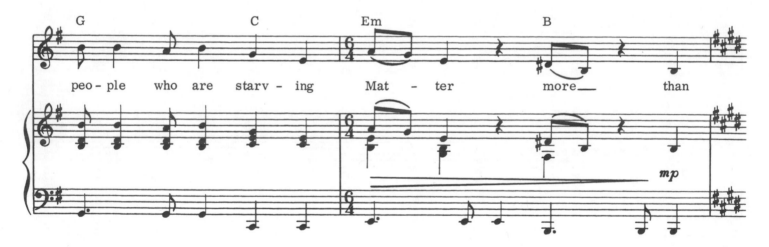

peo-ple who are starv-ing Mat - ter more _____ than

D.S. al Coda

your_ feet and hair

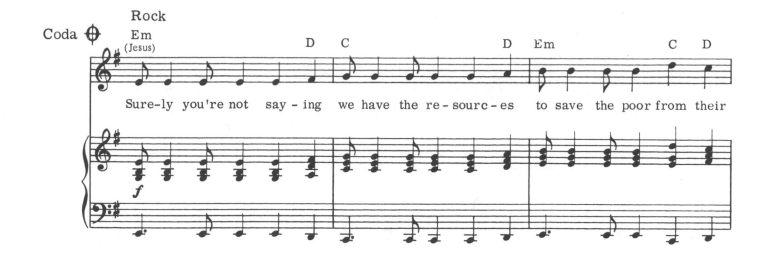

Surely you're not saying we have the resources to save the poor from their

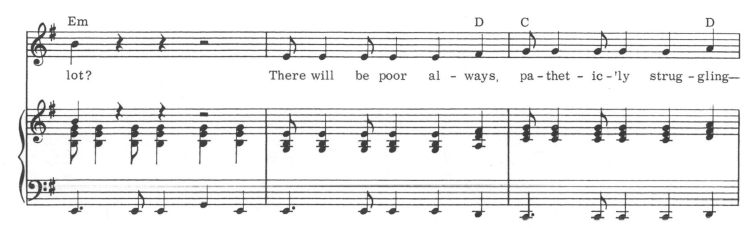

lot? There will be poor always, pathetic'ly struggling—

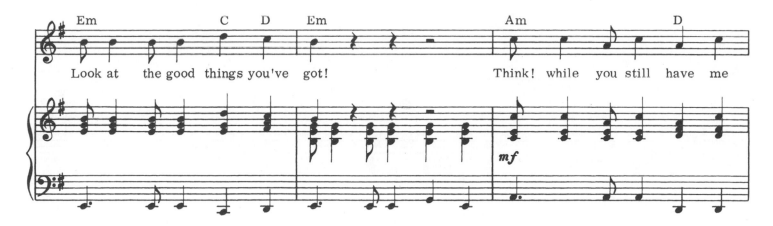

Look at the good things you've got! Think! while you still have me

Move! while you still see me You'll be lost— You'll be so so

Light Rock

(Mary Magdalene)

Sleep and I shall soothe you, calm you and a - noint you

Myrrh for your hot fore - head oh then you'll feel Ev - 'ry - thing's al - right yes

ev - 'ry - thing's fine And it's cool___ and the oint - ment's

sweet _____ For the fire__ in your head and feet _____ Close your

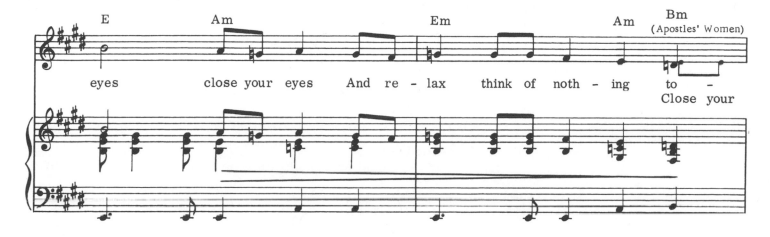

eyes   close your eyes   And re - lax   think of noth - ing   to -
                                                                Close your

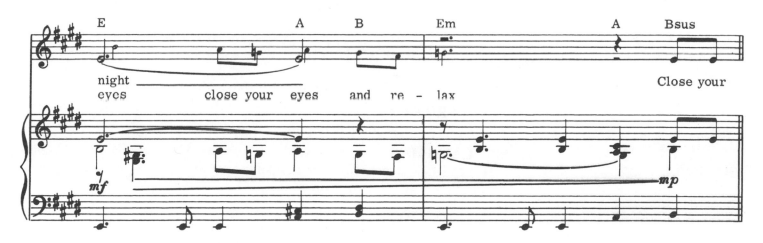

night _____
eyes   close your eyes   and re - lax
                                                    Close your

Hard Rock
Repeat many times, crescendo to f then fade

eyes   close your eyes   and re - lax   Close your
Ev - 'ry - thing's al - right   yes   ev - 'ry - thing's all   right   yes

THIS JESUS MUST DIE

Jerusalem, Sunday

PRIEST 1

Good Caiaphas the council waits for you
The Pharisees and priests are here for you

CAIAPHAS

Ah gentlemen—you know why we are here
We've not much time and quite a problem here

MOB outside

Hosanna! Superstar!

ANNAS

Listen to that howling mob of blockheads in the street!
A trick or two with lepers and the whole town's on its feet

ALL

He is dangerous

MOB outside

Jesus Christ Superstar—tell us that you're
who they say you are

ALL

He is dangerous

PRIEST 2

The man is in town right now to whip up some support

PRIEST 3

A rabble rousing mission that I think we must abort

ALL

He is dangerous!

MOB outside

Jesus Christ Superstar!

ALL

He is dangerous!

PRIEST 2

Look Caiaphas—they're right outside our yard

PRIEST 3

Quick Caiaphas—go call the Roman guard

CAIAPHAS

No wait—we need a more permanent solution
to our problem...

ANNAS

What then to do about Jesus of Nazareth
Miracle wonderman—hero of fools?

PRIEST 3

No riots, no army, no fighting, no slogans

CAIAPHAS

One thing I'll say for him—Jesus is cool

ANNAS

We dare not leave him to his own devices
His half-witted fans will get out of control

PRIEST 3

But how can we stop him? His glamour increases
By leaps every minute—he's top of the poll

CAIAPHAS

I see bad things arising—the crowd crown him king
Which the Romans would ban
I see blood and destruction, our elimination
because of one man
Blood and destruction because of one man

ALL

Because, because, because of one man

CAIAPHAS

Our elimination because of one man

ALL

Because, because, because of one, 'cause of one,
'cause of one man

PRIEST 3

What then to do about this Jesusmania?

ANNAS

How do we deal with the carpenter king?

PRIEST 3

Where do we start with a man who is bigger
Than John was when John did his Baptism thing?

CAIAPHAS

Fools! You have no perception!
The stakes we are gambling are frighteningly high!
We must crush him completely—
So like John before him, this Jesus must die
For the sake of the nation this Jesus must die

ALL

Must die, must die, this Jesus must die

CAIAPHAS

So like John before him, this Jesus must die

ALL

Must die, must die, this Jesus must, Jesus must,
Jesus must die!

HOSANNA

Words by TIM RICE
Music by ANDREW LLOYD WEBBER

Ho - san-na Hey - san-na San-na San-na Ho San-na

Hey San-na Ho San - na   Hey J C, J C won't you smile at me? San-na

Ho___ San-na Hey Su-per-star   Tell this rab-ble to be qui-et we an-

21

C, J C you're al – right by me San – na Ho__ San – na Hey Su – per-star

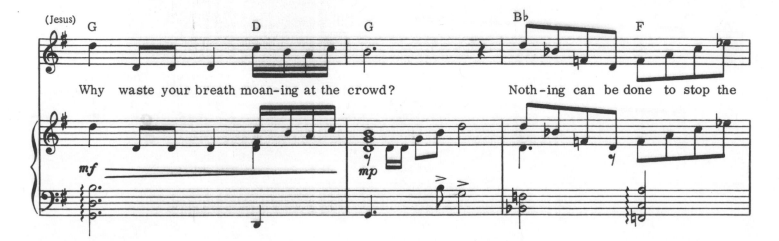

(Jesus) Why waste your breath moan-ing at the crowd? Noth-ing can be done to stop the

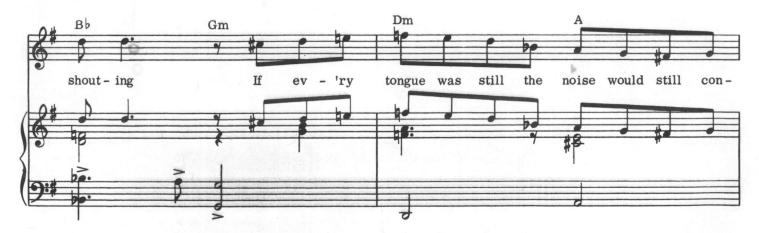

shout – ing If ev – 'ry tongue was still the noise would still con –

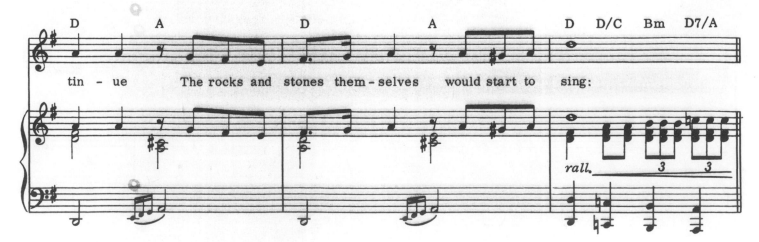

tin – ue The rocks and stones them-selves would start to sing:

Slowly and majestically

(Crowd, with Jesus)

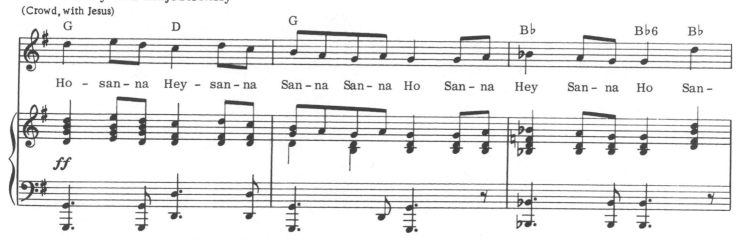

Ho — san — na Hey — san — na San — na San — na Ho San — na Hey San — na Ho San —

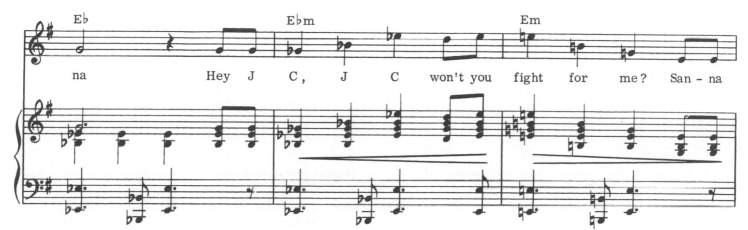

na Hey J C, J C won't you fight for me? San — na

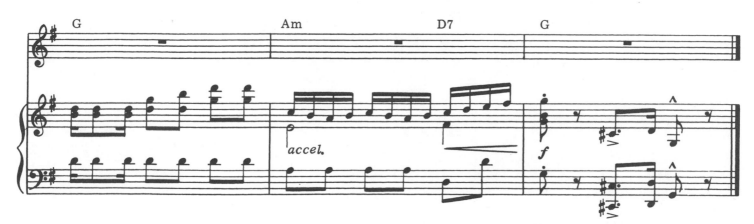

Ho_____ San — na Hey Su — per — star

SIMON ZEALOTES

CROWD

Christ you know I love you
Did you see I waved?
I believe in you and God
So tell me that I'm saved
Christ you know I love you
Did you see I waved?
I believe in you and God
So tell me that I'm saved
Jesus I am with you
Touch me touch me Jesus
Jesus I am on your side
Kiss me kiss me Jesus

SIMON ZEALOTES

Christ, what more do you need to convince you
That you've made it and you're easily as strong
As the filth from Rome who rape our country
And who've terrorized our people for so long?

CROWD

Christ you know I love you
Did you see I waved?
I believe in you and God
So tell me that I'm saved
Christ you know I love you
Did you see I waved?
I believe in you and God
So tell me that I'm saved
Jesus I am with you
Touch me touch me Jesus
Jesus I am on your side
Kiss me kiss me Jesus

SIMON ZEALOTES

There must be over fifty thousand
Screaming love and more for you
Everyone of fifty thousand
Would do whatever you ask him to
Keep them yelling their devotion
But add a touch of hate at Rome
You will rise to a greater power
We will win ourselves a home
You'll get the power and the glory
For ever and ever and ever
Amen! Amen!

POOR JERUSALEM

JESUS

Neither you Simon, nor the fifty thousand
Nor the Romans, nor the Jews, nor Judas nor the Twelve,
Nor the Priests, nor the Scribes
Nor doomed Jerusalem itself,
Understand what power is
Understand what glory is
Understand at all... understand at all
If you knew all that I knew, my poor Jerusalem
You'd see the truth, but you close your eyes
But you close your eyes
While you live your troubles are many, poor Jerusalem
To conquer death you only have to die
You only have to die

PILATE'S DREAM

Words by TIM RICE
Music by ANDREW LLOYD WEBBER

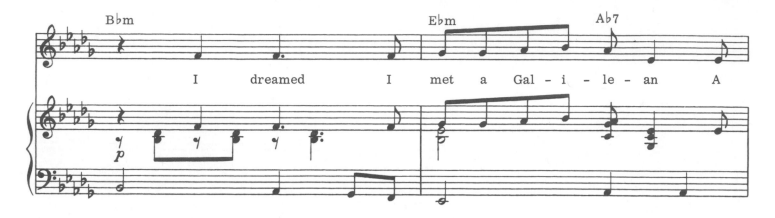

I dreamed I met a Gal-i-le-an A

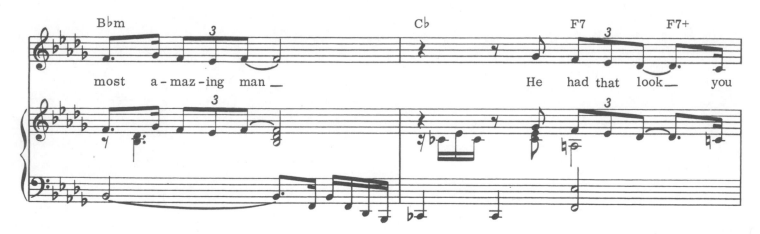

most a-maz-ing man ___ He had that look ___ you

ver-y rare-ly find The haunt-ing hunt-ed

kind   I asked him to say   what had hap-pened

How it all be-gan   I asked a - gain ___ he

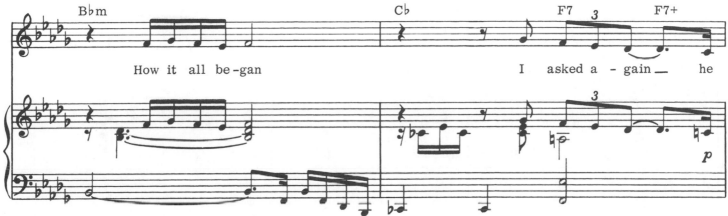

nev-er said a word   As if he had-n't heard

And   next   the room   was full   of   wild   and an-gry men

They seemed to hate this man — they fell on him and then They dis-ap-peared a-gain Then I saw thou-sands of mil-lions Cry-ing for this man — And then I heard them men-tion-ing my name And leav-ing me the blame

THE TEMPLE

The Temple
MONEYLENDERS AND MERCHANTS

Roll on up—for my price is down
Come on in—for the best in town
Take your pick of the finest wine
Lay your bets on this bird of mine
Roll on up—for my price is down
Come on in—for the best in town
Take your pick of the finest wine
Lay your bets on this bird of mine
Name your price I got everything
Come and buy it's all going fast
Borrow cash on the finest terms
Hurry now while stocks still last.

JESUS

My temple should be a house of prayer
But you have made it a den of thieves
Get out! Get out!
My time is almost through
Little left to do
After all I've tried for three years, seems like thirty
Seems like thirty

CROWD

See my eyes I can hardly see
See me stand I can hardly walk
I believe you can make me whole
See my tongue I can hardly talk
See my skin I'm a mass of blood
See my legs I can hardly stand
I believe you can make me well
See my purse I'm a poor poor man
Will you touch will you mend me Christ
Won't you touch will you heal me Christ
Will you kiss you can cure me Christ
Won't you kiss won't you pay me Christ

JESUS

There's too many of you—don't push me
There's too little of me—don't crowd me
Heal yourselves!

EVERYTHING'S ALRIGHT

MARY MAGDALENE

Try not to get worried try not to turn on to
Problems that upset you oh don't you know
Everything's alright yes everything's fine

JESUS

And I think I shall sleep well tonight
Let the world turn without me tonight

MARY MAGDALENE

Close your eyes close your eyes
And forget all about us tonight

I DON'T KNOW HOW TO LOVE HIM

Words by TIM RICE
Music by ANDREW LLOYD WEBBER

Slowly, Tenderly and Very Expressively

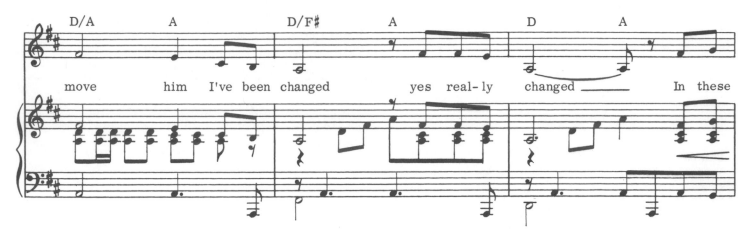

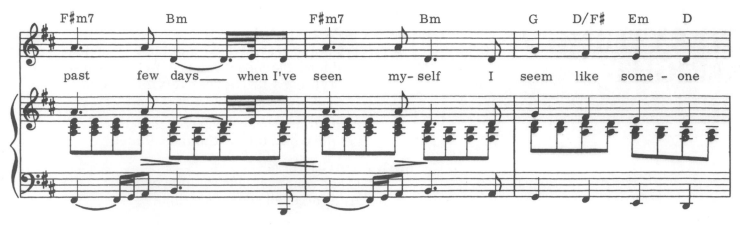

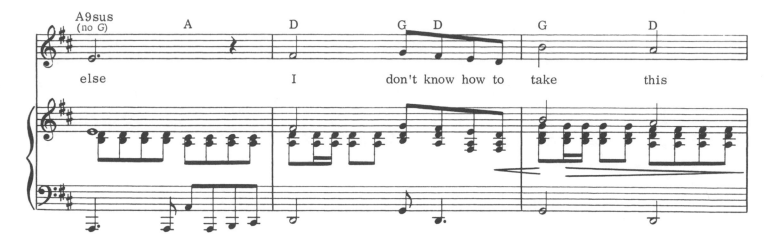

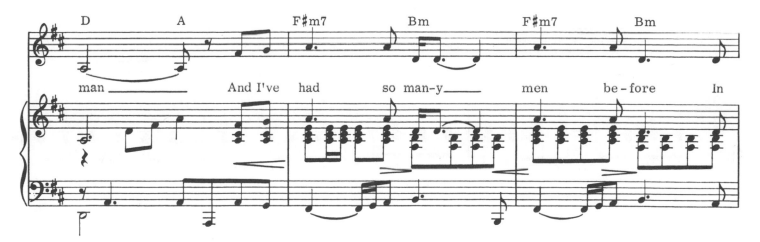

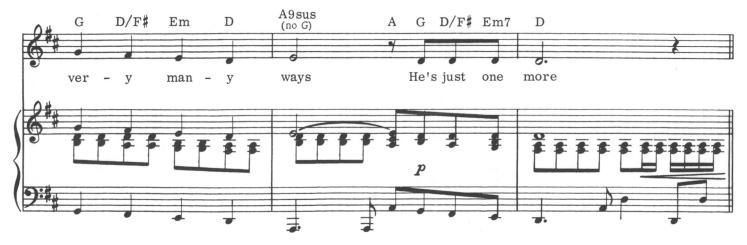

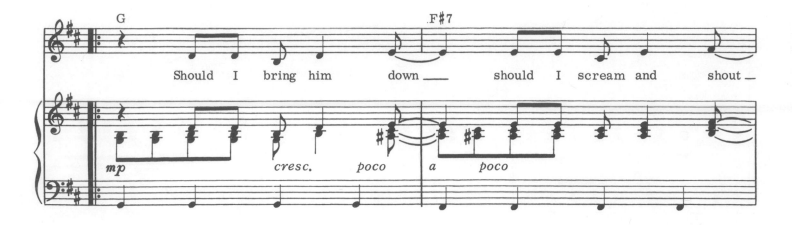

Should I bring him down _____ should I scream and shout _____

_____ Should I speak of love _____ let my feel-ings out? _____ I nev-er thought I'd

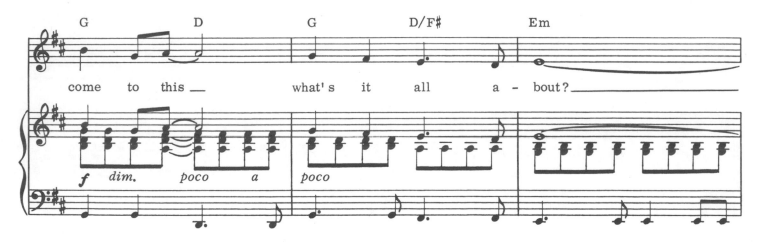

come to this _____ what's it all a - bout? _____

_____ Don't you think it's rath-er fun — ny
Yet if he said he loved me

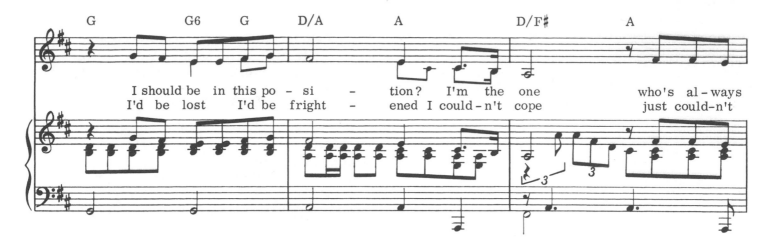

I should be in this po — si — tion? I'm the one who's al — ways
I'd be lost I'd be fright — ened I could — n't cope just could — n't

been _____ So calm so cool, no lov — er's fool
cope _____ I'd turn my head I'd back a — way I

Run — ning ev — 'ry show He scares me so _____
would — n't want to know He scares me

1.

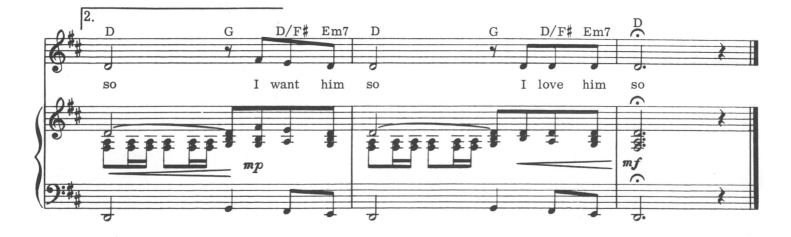

2.

so I want him so I love him so

DAMNED FOR ALL TIME

JUDAS

Now if I help you it matters that you see
These sordid kind of things are coming hard to me
It's taken me some time to work out what to do
I weighed the whole thing up before I came to you
I have no thought at all about my own reward
I really didn't come here of my own accord
Just don't say I'm
Damned for all time

I came because I had to I'm the one who saw
Jesus can't control it like he did before
And furthermore I know that Jesus thinks so too
Jesus wouldn't mind that I was here with you
I have no thought at all about my own reward
I really didn't come here of my own accord
Just don't say I'm
Damned for all time

Annas you're a friend a wordly man and wise
Caiaphas my friend I know you sympathise
Why are we the prophets? Why are we the ones?
Who see the sad solution—know what must be done
I have no thought at all about my own reward
I really didn't come here of my own accord
Just don't say I'm
Damned for all time

ANNAS

Cut the protesting forget the excuses
We want information get up off the floor

CAIAPHAS

We have the papers we need to arrest him
You know his movements—we know the law

ANNAS

Your help in this matter won't go unrewarded

CAIAPHAS

We'll pay you in silver—cash on the nail
We just need to know where the soldiers can find him

ANNAS

With no crowd around him

CAIAPHAS

Then we can't fail

BLOOD MONEY

JUDAS

I don't need your blood money!

CAIAPHAS

Oh that doesn't matter our expenses are good

JUDAS

I don't want your blood money!

ANNAS

But you might as well take it—we think that you should

CAIAPHAS

Think of the things you can do with that money
Choose any charity—give to the poor
We've noted your motives—we've noted your feelings
This isn't blood money—it's a fee nothing
Fee nothing, fee nothing more.

JUDAS

On Thursday night you'll find him where you want him
Far from the crowds in the Garden of Gethsemane

CHOIR

Well done Judas
Good old Judas

THE LAST SUPPER

Words by TIM RICE
Music by ANDREW LLOYD WEBBER

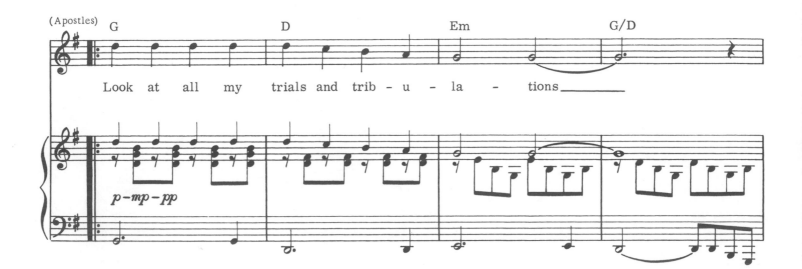

(Apostles)

Look at all my trials and trib - u - la - tions _____

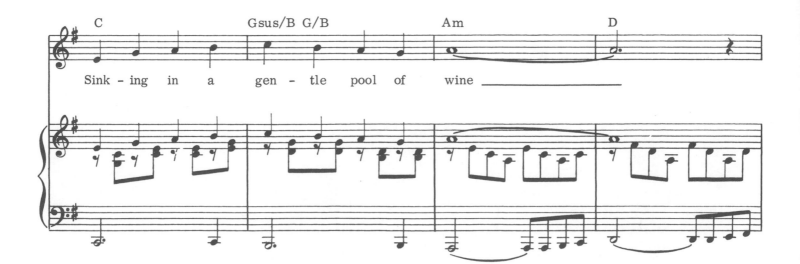

Sink - ing in a gen - tle pool of wine _____

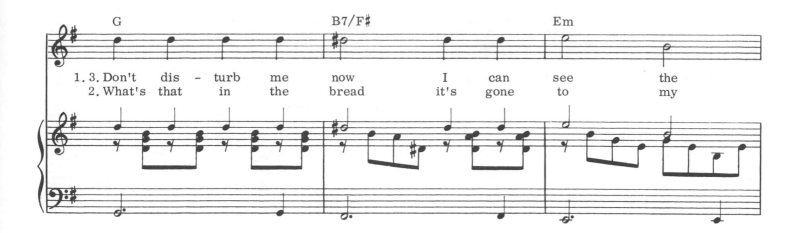

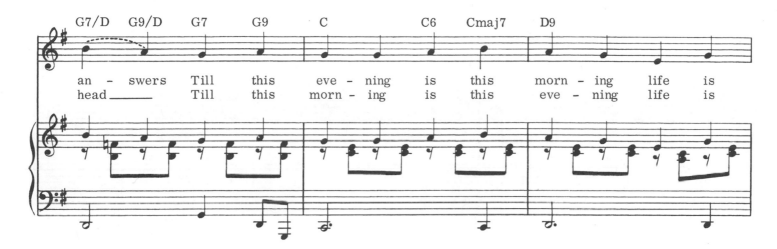

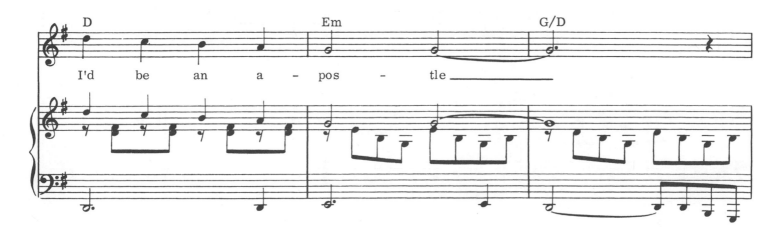

3rd time – gradually fade out

Knew that I would make it if I tried _____

Then when we re - tire we can write the

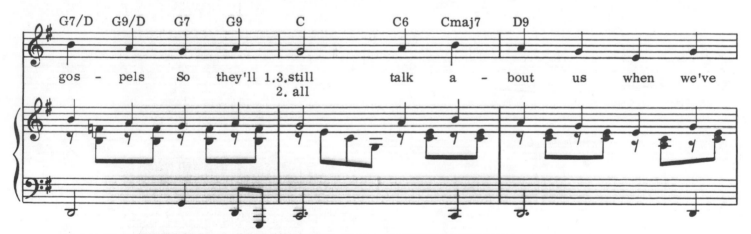

gos - pels So they'll 1.3.still talk a - bout us when we've
                          2. all

1.2. died _____

3. died. _____

Chords: C | Gsus/B G/B | Am | D | G | B7/F# | Em | G7/D G9/D G7 G9 | C | C6 Cmaj7 D9 | G | D7 | D7 | G

rall.   *pppp*

38

THE LAST SUPPER

JESUS

The end...
Is just a little harder when brought about by friends
For all you care this wine could be my blood
For all you care this bread could be my body
The end!
This my blood you drink
This is my body you eat
If you would remember me when you eat and drink...
I must be mad thinking I'll be remembered—yes
I must be out of my head!
Look at your blank faces! My name will mean nothing
Ten minutes after I'm dead!
One of you denies me
One of you betrays me—

APOSTLES

Not I! Who would? Impossible!

JESUS

Peter will deny me in just a few hours
Three times will deny me—and that's not all I see
One of you here dining, one of my twelve chosen
Will leave to betray me—

JUDAS

Cut out the dramatics! You know very well who—

JESUS   **JUDAS**

Why don't you go do it?   You want me to do it!

JESUS   **JUDAS**

Hurry they are waiting   If you knew why I do it...

JESUS   **JUDAS**

I don't care why you do it! To think I admired you
                             For now I despise you

JESUS

You liar—you Judas

JUDAS

You want me to do it!
What if I just stayed here
And ruined your ambition?
Christ you deserve it!

JESUS

Hurry you fool, hurry and go,
Save me your speeches, I don't want to know—Go!

APOSTLES (Music repeats   page 36)
JUDAS

You sad pathetic man—see where you've brought us to
Our ideals die around us all because of you
And now the saddest cut of all—
Someone has to turn you in
Like a common criminal, like a wounded animal
A jaded mandarin
A jaded mandarin
A jaded faded mandarin

JESUS

Get out! They're waiting! They're waiting for you!

JUDAS

Everytime I look at you I don't understand
Why you let the things you did get so out of hand
You'd have managed better if you'd had it planned—

APOSTLES (Music repeats   page 36)
JESUS

Will no-one stay awake with me?
Peter? John? James?
Will none of you wait with me?
Peter? John? James?

I ONLY WANT TO SAY
(GETHSEMANE)

Words by TIM RICE
Music by ANDREW LLOYD WEBBER

not as sure___ As when we start-ed Then I was in - spired

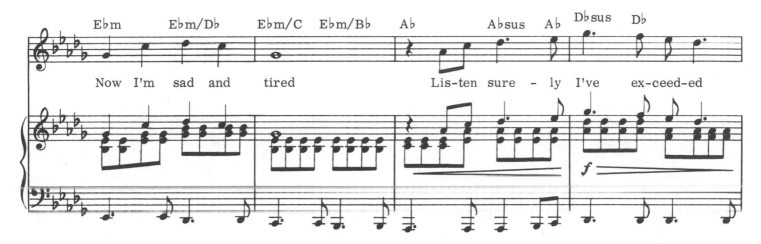

Now I'm sad and tired Lis-ten sure - ly I've ex-ceed-ed

ex-pec-ta-tions Tried for three years seems like thir-ty

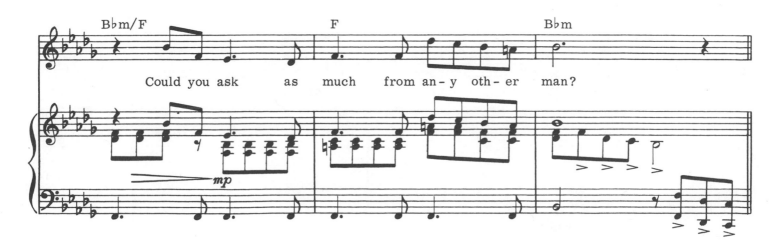

Could you ask as much from an-y oth-er man?

If I die what will_ be my re - ward? If I die what will_ be my re - ward?

I'd have to know I have_ to know my Lord_ I'd have to know I'd have_ to know my Lord_

Vocal: *ad lib.* -

Why should I die? Why should I die?

Can you show me now that I would not be killed in vain?

Show me just a lit - tle of your om - ni - pres - ent brain

Show me there's a rea - son for your want - ing me to die You're

far too keen on where and how and not so hot on why

Al - right I'll die! Just watch

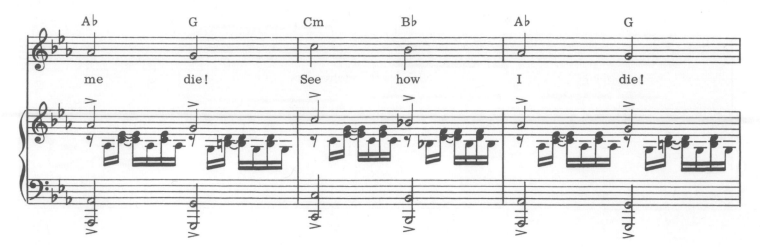

me die! See how I die!

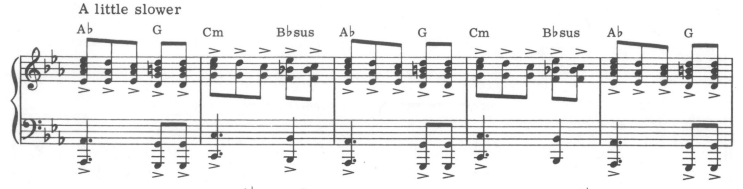

See how I die!

A little slower

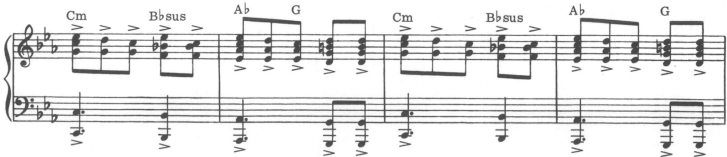

Tempo I

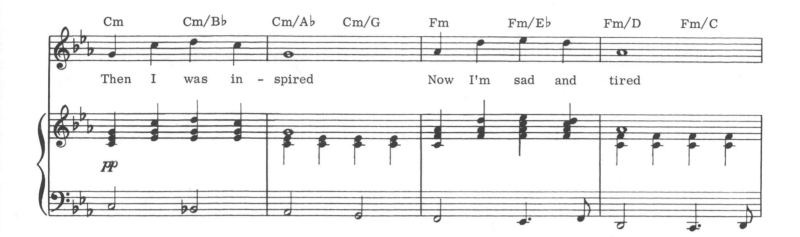

Then I was in-spired Now I'm sad and tired

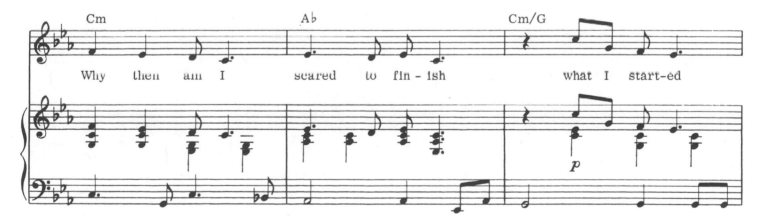

Af-ter all I've tried for three years seems like nine-ty

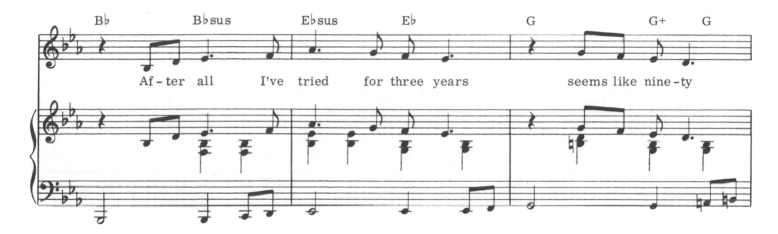

Why then am I scared to fin-ish what I start-ed

Majestically

What you start-ed —— I did-n't start it God thy will is

hard _____ But you hold ev - 'ry card

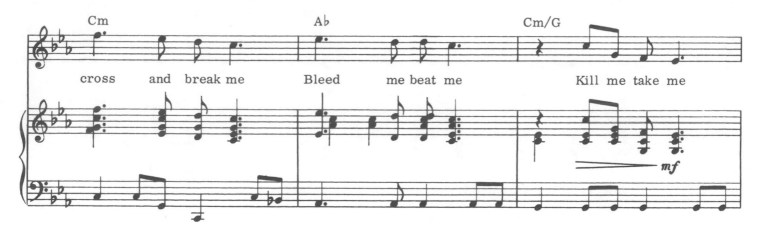

I will drink your cup of poi - son, nail me to your

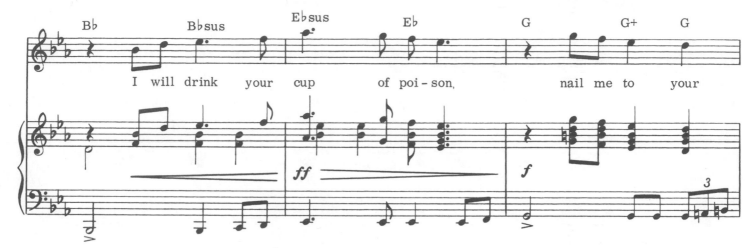

cross and break me Bleed me beat me Kill me take me

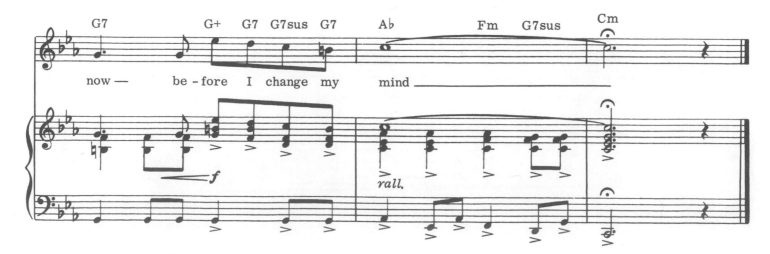

now — be - fore I change my mind _____

THE ARREST

JUDAS

There he is! They're all asleep—the fools!

JESUS

Judas—must you betray me with a kiss?

PETER

What's the buzz? Tell me what's happening

PETER AND APOSTLES

What's the buzz? Tell me what's happening
Hang on Lord we're gonna fight for you

JESUS

Put away your sword
Don't you know that it's all over?
It was nice but now it's gone
Why are you obsessed with fighting?
Stick to fishing from now on

CROWD

Tell me Christ how you feel tonight
Do you plan to put up a fight?
Do you feel that you've had the breaks?
What would you say were your big mistakes?
Do you think that you may retire?
Did you think you would get much higher?
How do you view your coming trial?
Have your men proved at all worthwhile?

Come with us to see Caiaphas
You'll just love the High Priest's house
You'll just love seeing Caiaphas
You'll just die in the High Priest's house

Come on God this is not like you
Let us know what you're gonna do
You know what your supporters feel
You'll escape in the final reel
Tell me Christ how you feel tonight
Do you plan to put up a fight?
Do you feel that you've had the breaks?
What would you say were your big mistakes?

Come with us to see Caiaphas
You'll just love the High Priest's house
You'll just love seeing Caiaphas
You'll just die in the High Priest's house

Now we have him! Now we have got him!

CAIAPHAS

Jesus you must realise the serious charges facing you
You say you're the Son of God in all your handouts—
    well is it true?

JESUS

That's what you say—you say that I am

ANNAS

There you have it gentlemen—
    what more evidence do we need?
Judas thank you for the victim—
    stay a while and you'll see it bleed!

CROWD

Now we have him! Now we have got him!
Take him to Pilate!

PETER'S DENIAL

MAID BY THE FIRE

I think I've seen you somewhere—I remember
You were with that man they took away
I recognise your face

PETER

You've got the wrong man lady I don't know him
And I wasn't where he was tonight—never near the place

SOLDIER

That's strange for I am sure I saw you with him
You were right by his side and yet you denied—

PETER

I tell you I was never ever with him

OLD MAN

But I saw you too—it looked just like you

PETER

I don't know him!

MARY MAGDALENE

Peter—don't you know what you have said
You've gone and cut him dead

PETER

I had to do it don't you see?
Or else they'd go for me

MARY MAGDALENE

It's what he told us you would do—
I wonder how he knew...

PILATE AND CHRIST

PILATE Friday

Who is this broken man cluttering up my hallway?
Who is this unfortunate?

SOLDIER

Someone Christ—King of the Jews

PILATE

Oh so this is Jesus Christ, I am really quite surprised
You look so small—not a king at all
We all know that you are news—but are you king?
King of the Jews?

JESUS

That's what you say

PILATE

What do you mean by that?
That is not an answer
You're deep in trouble friend—
Someone Christ—King of the Jews
How can someone in your state be so cool about your fate?
An amazing thing—this silent king
Since you come from Galilee then you need not come to me
You're Herod's race! You're Herod's case!

MOB

Ho-ho Sanna Hey Sanna Sanna Sanna Ho
Sanna Hey Sanna Ho and how
Hey JC, JC please explain to me
You had everything where is it now?

KING HEROD'S SONG

Words by TIM RICE
Music by ANDREW LLOYD WEBBER

Je - sus I am o - ver - joyed to meet you face to face

You've been get - ting quite a name all a - round the place ___

Heal - ing crip - ples rais - ing from the dead And

now I un-der-stand you're God at least that's what you've said

So

Moderato, Ragtime style

you are the Christ___ you're the great Je - sus Christ___
you are the Christ___ you're the great Je - sus Christ___

Prove to me that you're di - vine___ Change my wa - ter in - to wine___ That's
Prove to me that you're no fool___ Walk a - cross my swim-ming pool___ If you

all you need do___ and I'll know it's all true___
do that for me___ then I'll let you go free___

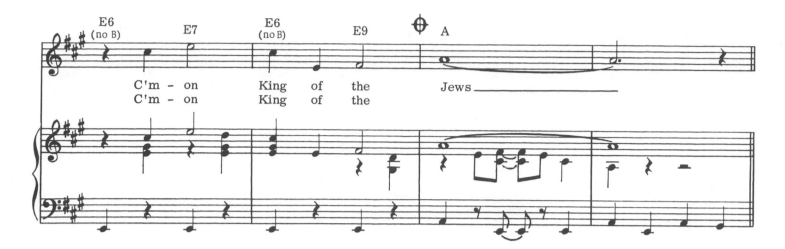

C'm - on   King of the   Jews _____
C'm - on   King of the

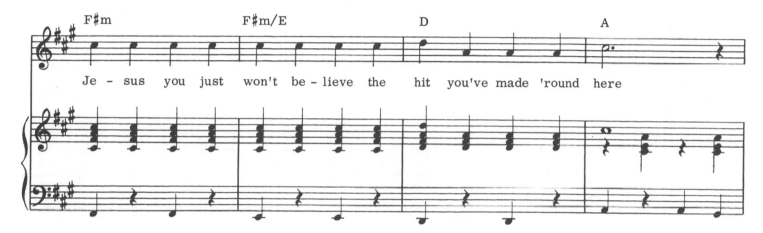

Je - sus you just won't be - lieve the   hit you've made 'round here

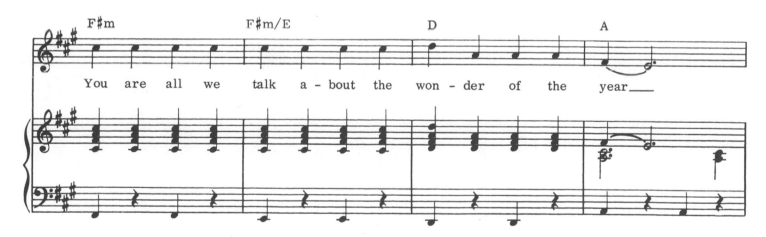

You are all we   talk a - bout the won - der of the   year___

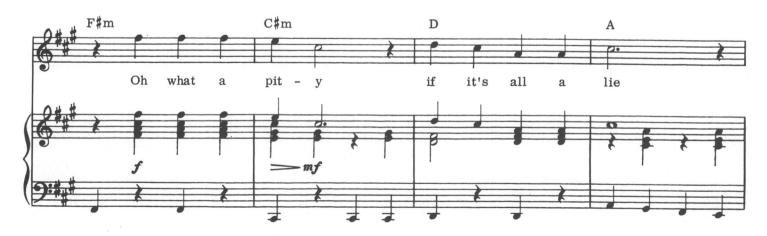

Oh what a pit - y   if it's all a   lie

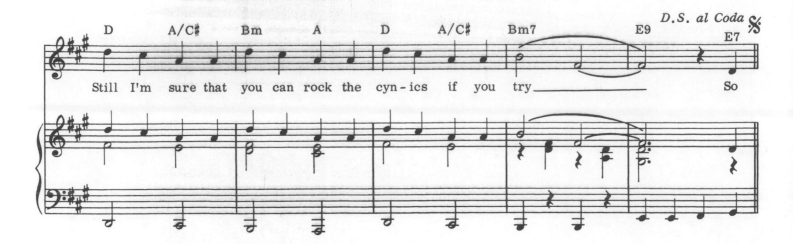

Still I'm sure that you can rock the cyn-ics if you try_____ So

D.S. al Coda

Coda

Jews._____ I on-ly ask things I'd ask

an-y su-per-star What is it that you have got that

puts you where you are?___ I am wait-ing yes

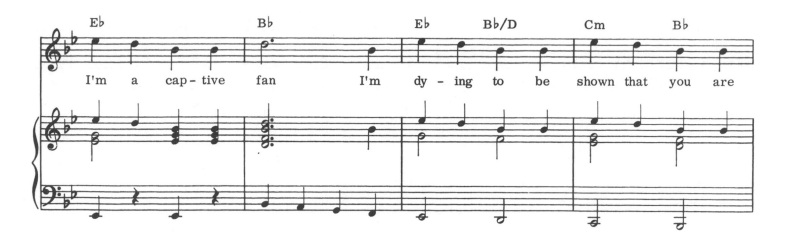

I'm a cap-tive fan I'm dy-ing to be shown that you are

not just an-y man _____ So if you are the Christ_ yes the

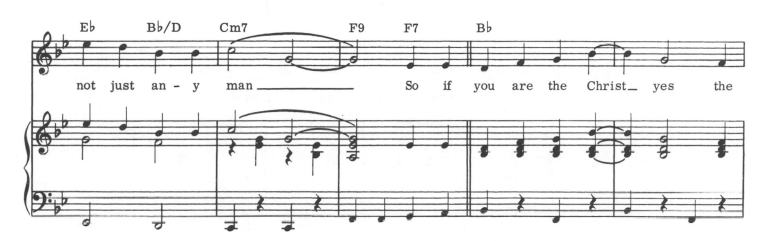

great Je-sus Christ___ Feed my house-hold with this bread___

you can do it on your head___ Or has some-thing gone wrong?__ Why do

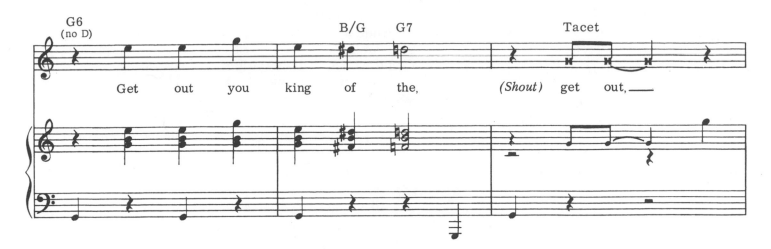

Get out you king of the, *(Shout)* get out, ___

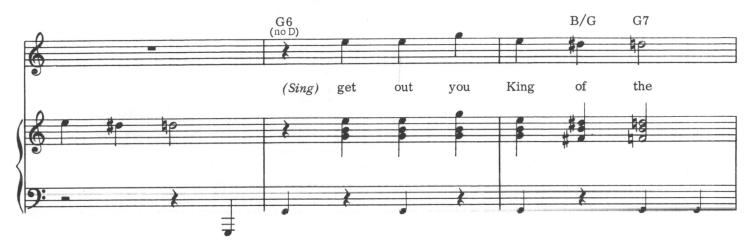

(Sing) get out you King of the

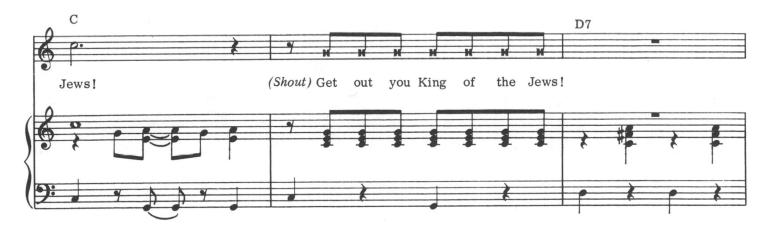

Jews!   *(Shout)* Get out you King of the Jews!

Get out ___ of my life!

JUDAS' DEATH

JUDAS

My God! I saw him—he looked three-quarters dead!
And he was so bad I had to turn my head
You beat him so hard that he was bent and lame
And I know who everybody's gonna blame
I don't believe he knows I acted for our good
I'd save him all this suffering if I could
Don't believe...our good...save him...if I could

PRIEST 3

Cut the confessions forget the excuses
I don't understand why you're filled with remorse
All that you've said has come true with a vengeance
The mob turned against him—you backed the right horse

CAIAPHAS

What you have done will be the saving of Israel
You'll be remembered forever for this
And not only that you've been paid for your efforts
Pretty good wages for one little kiss

JUDAS

Christ! I know you can't hear me
But I only did what you wanted me to
Christ! I'd sell out the nation
For I have been saddled with the murder of you
I have been spattered with innocent blood
I shall be dragged through the slime and the mud
I have been spattered with innocent blood
I shall be dragged through the slime and the mud!
I don't know how to love him.
I don't know why he moves me
He's a man—he's just a man
He's not a king—he's just the same
As anyone I know
He scares me so
When he's cold and dead will he let me be?
Does he love me too? Does he care for me?
My mind is darkness now—My God I am sick I've been used
And you knew all the time
God! I'll never ever know why you chose me for your crime
For your foul bloody crime
You have murdered me! You have murdered me!

CHOIR

Poor old Judas
So long Judas

TRIAL BEFORE PILATE (Including the 39 LASHES)

PILATE

And so the king is once again my guest
And why is this? Was Herod unimpressed?

CAIAPHAS

We turn to Rome to sentence Nazareth
We have no law to put a man to death
We need him crucified—it's all you have to do
We need him crucified—it's all you have to do

PILATE

Talk to me Jesus Christ
You have been brought here—manacled, beaten
By your own people—do you have the first idea
    why you deserve it?
Listen, King of the Jews
Where is your kingdom?
Look at me—am I a Jew?

JESUS

I have got no kingdom in this world—
    I'm through, through, through

MOB

Talk to me Jesus Christ

JESUS

There may be a kingdom for me somewhere—if I only knew

PILATE

Then you're a king?

JESUS

It's you that say I am
I look for truth and find that I get damned

PILATE

But what is truth? Is truth unchanging law?
We both have truths—are mine the same as yours?

MOB

Crucify him!

PILATE

What do you mean? You'd crucify your king?

MOB

We have no king but Caesar!

PILATE

He's done no wrong—no not the slightest thing

MOB

We have no king but Caesar! Crucify him!

PILATE

I see no reason—I find no evil
This man is harmless so why does he upset you?
He's just misguided—thinks he's important
But to keep you vultures happy I shall flog him

MOB

Crucify him!

(Thirty nine lashes)

PILATE

Where are you from Jesus? What do you want Jesus?
    Tell me
You've got to be careful—you could be dead soon—
    could well be
Why do you not speak when I have your life in my hands?
How can you stay quiet? I don't believe you understand

59

TRIAL BEFORE PILATE
(Including The 39 Lashes)

JESUS

You have nothing in your hands
Any power you have comes to you from far beyond
Everything is fixed and you can't change it

PILATE

You're a fool Jesus Christ—how can I help you?

MOB

Pilate! Crucify him!
Remember Caesar—you have a duty
To keep the peace so crucify him!
Remember Caesar—you'll be demoted, you'll be deported
Crucify him!

PILATE

Don't let me stop your great self-destruction
Die if you want to you misguided martyr
I wash my hands of your demolition
Die if you want to you innocent puppet!

SUPERSTAR

Words by TIM RICE
Music by ANDREW LLOYD WEBBER

Maestoso

Moderato (Freely — 'Soul' style)
(Voice of Judas)

Ev-'ry-time I look at you I don't un-der-stand __ Why you let the things you did get
Tell me what you think a-bout your friends at the top __ Who d'you think be-sides your-self's the

so out of hand __ You'd have man-aged bet-ter if vou'd had __ it planned __
pick of the crop? __ Bud-dah was he where it's at? Is he where you are? __

Why'd you choose such a back-ward time and such a strange land? __
Could Ma-hom-et __ move a moun-tain or was that just P R ? __

If you'd come to-day you would have reached a whole na - tion
Did you mean to die like that? Was that a mis-take____ or

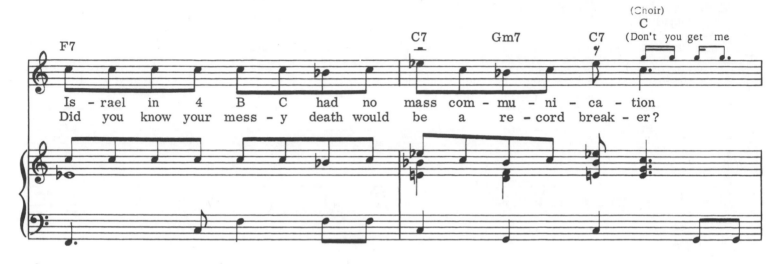

Is - rael in 4 B C had no mass com - mu - ni - ca - tion
Did you know your mess - y death would be a re - cord break - er?

(Choir)
(Don't you get me

wrong)
Don't you get me wrong____

(Don't you get me
Don't you get me wrong____

wrong now)

(Don't you get me

wrong)
Don't you get me wrong____

(Don't you get me
Don't you get me wrong____

wrong now)

(I on - ly want to

On – ly want to know___   On – ly want to know___

On – ly want to know___   On – ly want to know___   Je – sus Christ___

Je – sus Christ___ Who are you? What have you sac – ri – ficed?___ Je – sus Christ___

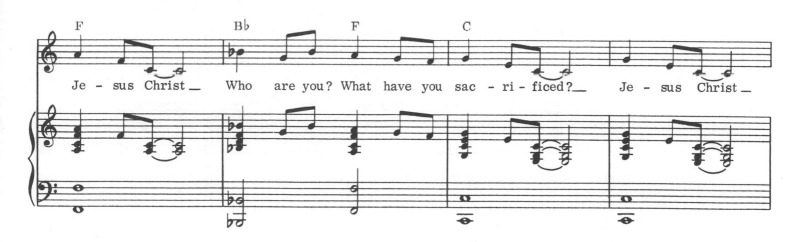

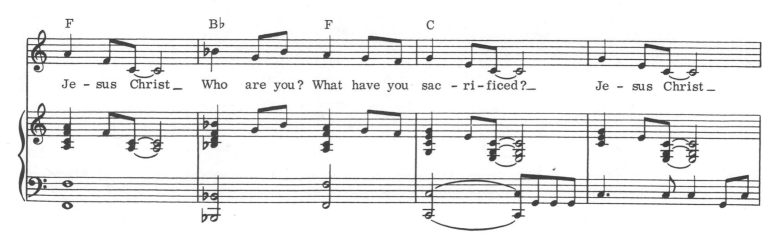

Je – sus Christ___ Who are you? What have you sac – ri – ficed?___ Je – sus Christ___